REVISITING

THE PIANO

Available for the first time for solo piano:
four arrangements from the soundtrack
plus the two favourite themes from
the award-winning film by Jane Campion

MICHAEL NYMAN

Exclusive distributors:
Hal Leonard
7777 West Bluemound Road
Milwaukee, WI 53213
Email: info@halleonard.com

Hal Leonard Europe Limited
42 Wigmore Street
Marylebone, London, W1U 2RY
Email: info@halleonardeurope.com

Hal Leonard Australia Pty. Ltd.
4 Lentara Court
Cheltenham, Victoria, 3192 Australia
Email: info@halleonard.com.au

This book © Copyright 1998,
Chester Music.
ISBN 0-7119-6884-5
Order No. CH61411

Book design by Michael Bell Design
Music processing by New Notations.
Photographs courtesy of Ronald Grant
Archive and EMI Classics and Virgin
Venture (Sheila Rock).

Printed in the EU

Chester Music

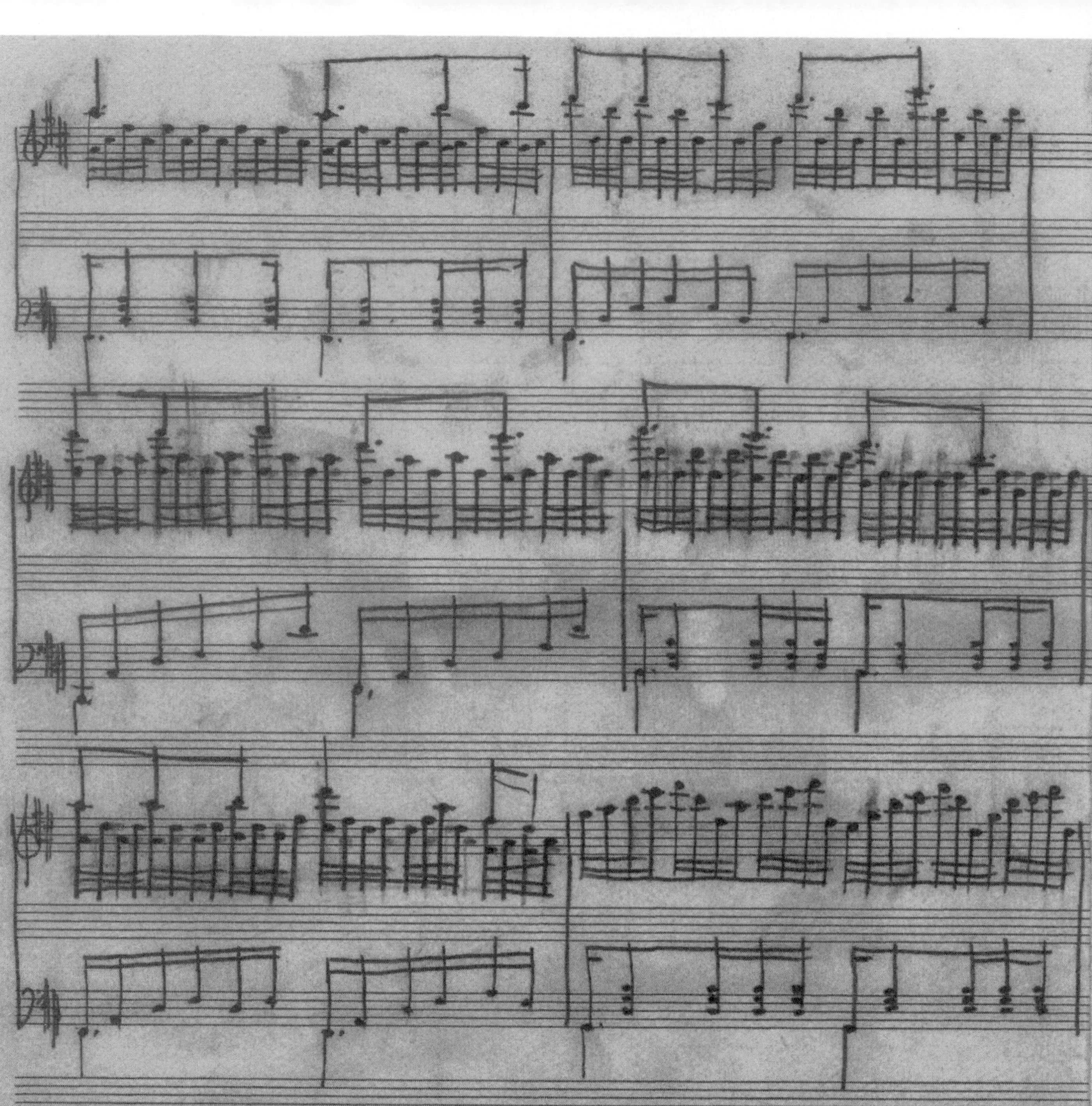

DEAR HOLLY

Very excited by your reactions – can't wait to hear you play it all. As regards [M10] play the melody as you feel fit, and try the above solution for the top 3 staves of page 4 – it's stronger and lies under the hand better. If it's still difficult then maybe – no, I really want the effect of the sustained and the hysterical in the right hand!!

Sorry about the smallness of the notes – this is the only manuscript paper I have with me.

→ maybe like bar 7 of this page (4): fast notes in left hand, 16th notes in right hand.

PAN-A3 18 STAVE

I also look forward to hearing the Holly Special on 8 Jan!

HAPPY NEW YEAR

Manuscript sketch from *The Piano* and note to Holly Hunter

REVISITING THE PIANO
MICHAEL NYMAN

When Michael Nyman published his study Experimental Music: John Cage and Beyond (1974), he could hardly have foreseen his own contribution to that 'beyond'. Rejecting the orthodoxies of British modernism, Nyman had abandoned composition in 1964, working instead as a musicologist, editing Purcell and Handel, and collecting folk music in Romania. Later he became a music critic, in which capacity he was the first to apply the word 'minimalism' to music, in a 1968 review for the Spectator of Cornelius Cardew's The Great Digest.

That same year, a chance encounter with a BBC broadcast of Steve Reich's *Come Out* opened his ears to further possibilities. A route back to composition was emerging. He wrote the libretto for Harrison Birtwistle's 1969 'dramatic pastoral' *Down by the Greenwood Side*. In 1977, Birtwistle, by now Musical Director of the National Theatre, commissioned him to provide arrangements of 18th-century Venetian songs for the production of Carlo Goldoni's play *Il Campiello*, to be performed by what Nyman describes as 'the loudest street band' he could imagine: rebecs, sackbuts and shawms alongside banjo, bass drum and saxophone.

Thrilled by the results, Nyman kept the Campiello Band together, now propelled by his own piano-playing. But a band needs repertoire, which Nyman set about providing, beginning with *In Re Don Giovanni*, a characteristic treatment of a 16-bar sequence by Mozart. Soon the band's line-up mutated, amplification was added, and the name changed to the Michael Nyman Band. This has been the laboratory in which Nyman has formulated his aesthetic, its sound world shaping a compositional style built around strong melodies, flexible, assertive rhythms and precisely articulated ensemble playing.

Besides concert-hall works, Nyman has written dozens of film scores for directors as diverse as Peter Greenaway, Jane Campion and Volker Schlöndorff; and pieces to accompany dance, a catwalk fashion show (*Yamamoto Perpetuo* for Japanese designer Yohji Yamamoto), the opening of a high-speed rail link (*MGV*, 1993) and a computer game (*Enemy Zero*). That acute sensitivity to occasion and context is enriched by a talent, shared with baroque composers, for refiguration: the 1995 *Concerto for Harpsichord and Strings* develops ideas previously encountered in *The Convertibility of Lute Strings* and *Tango for Tim*; the *Third String Quartet* lies behind the score for Christopher Hampton's 1996 movie *Carrington*.

At every turn Nyman has proved eminently practical. Not for him the ivory tower anguish of a tormented composer grappling with abstract systems, rather an openness to collaboration, a spry sense of humour, a highly literate imagination and an instant, instinctive ability to engage a highly diverse audience.

NICK KIMBERLEY

Other works by Michael Nyman

And Do They Do
Chamber ensemble
Score: CH61000 (parts available for hire)

Flugelhorn and Piano
Score: CH61001

For John Cage
Brass ensemble
Score: CH60866 (parts available for hire)

In Re Don Giovanni
String quartet
Score: CH61350 parts: CH61351

The Man who Mistook his Wife for a Hat
Chamber opera
Score: CH60918 vocal score: CH61224

Masque Arias
Brass quintet
Score: CH60999 parts: CH61238

Michael Nyman Film Music for Solo Piano
CH61400

Miserere
Treble solo/SATB
CH60022

On the Fiddle
Violin/cello and piano
CH61332

Out of the Ruins
SATB/opt organ
CH60272

The Piano
Gm MIDI book/disk pack
CH61065

Revisiting The Piano
Piano solo
CH61411

Shaping the Curve
Soprano saxophone and piano
CH61078

Six Celan Songs
Alto/counter tenor and ensemble
Score: CH60314 (parts available for hire)
Alto/counter tenor and piano
CH61412

Songs for Tony
Saxophone quartet
Score: CT55033 parts: CT55034

String Quartet No.1
Score: CH60850 parts: CH60975

String Quartet No.2
Score: CH60851 parts: CH60947

String Quartet No.3
Score: CH60865 parts: CH60976

String Quartet No.4
Score: CH61116 parts: CH61327

Time will Pronounce
Violin, cello and piano
Score: CH60798 Score and parts: CH61339

Viola and Piano
CH61263

Zoo Caprices
Violin solo
CH60852

For performance material,
general information and a complete work list
telephone 0171 432 4218.

Michael Nyman is published exclusively by
Chester Music.

Michael Nyman Filmography

Keep It Up Downstairs (1976)
Directed by Robert Young

1-100 (1977)
Directed by Peter Greenaway

A Walk Through H (1977)
Directed by Peter Greenaway

Vertical Features Remake (1978)
Directed by Peter Greenaway

The Falls (1980)
Directed by Peter Greenaway

The Draughtsman's Contract (1982)
Directed by Peter Greenaway

Brimstone and Treacle (1982)
Directed by Richard Loncraine

Frozen Music (1983)
Directed by Michael Eaton

Nelly's Version (1983)
Directed by Maurice Hatton

The Cold Room (1984)
Directed by James Dearden

A Zed and Two Noughts (1985)
Directed by Peter Greenaway

Ballet Méchanique (1986)
Directed by Fernand Léger

Drowning by Numbers (1987)
Directed by Peter Greenaway

The Cook, the Thief, his Wife and her Lover (1989)
Directed by Peter Greenaway

Monsieur Hire (1989)
Directed by Patrice Leconte

Prospero's Books (1990)
Directed by Peter Greenaway

Les Enfants Volants (1991)
Directed by Guillaume Nicloux

The Hairdresser's Husband (1991)
Directed by Patrice Leconte

Songbook (1992)
Directed by Volker Schlöndorff

The Piano (1992)
Directed by Jane Campion

Six Days, Six Nights (A La Folie) (1994)
Directed by Diane Kurys

Carrington (1994)
Directed by Christopher Hampton

The Diary Of Anne Frank (1995)
Produced by Seiya Araki

The Ogre (1996)
Directed by Volker Schlöndorff

Gattaca (1997)
Directed by Andrew Niccol

REVISITING THE PIANO

1. BIG MY SECRET

Molto adagio con rubato ♪ = 50 - 64

MICHAEL NYMAN

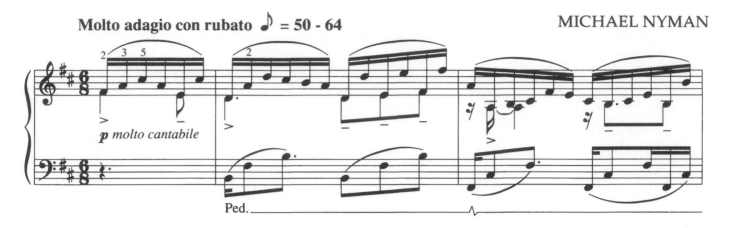

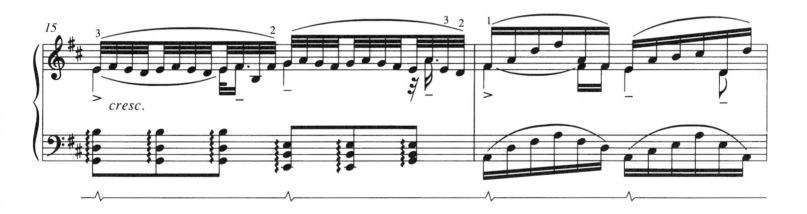

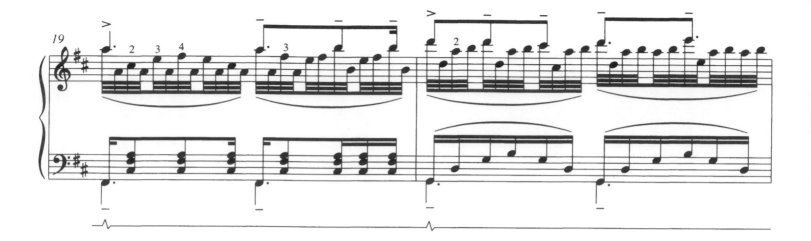

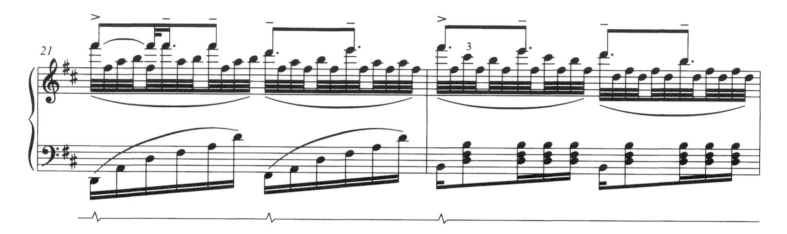

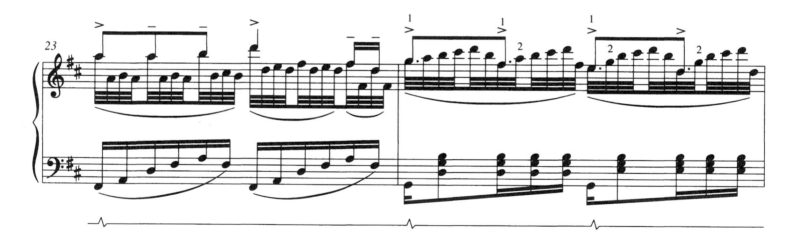

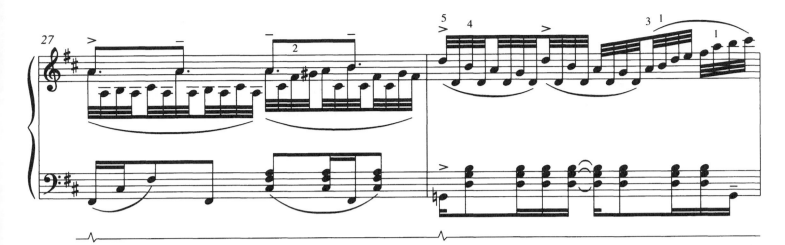

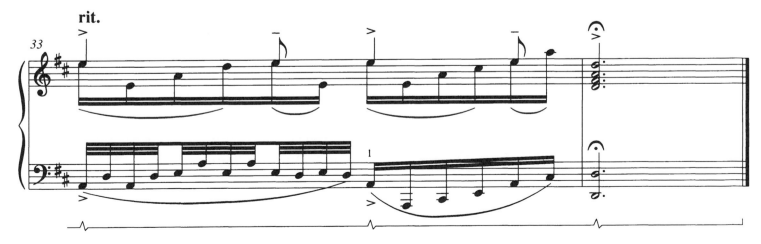

2. HERE TO THERE

* If required, LH may assist RH where indicated.

3. LOST AND FOUND

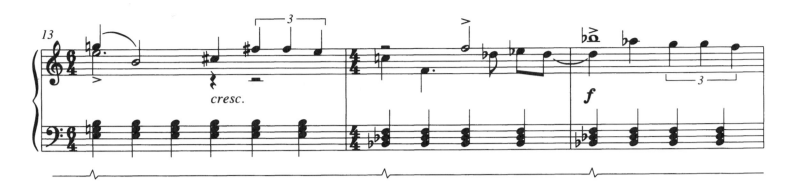

4. THE EMBRACE

5. ALL IMPERFECT THINGS

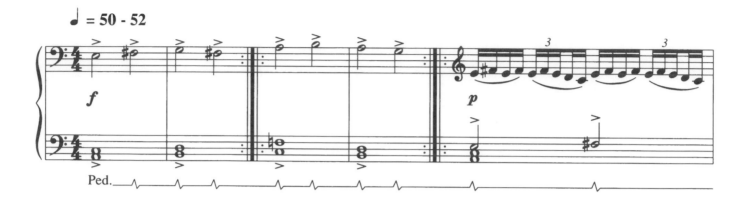

6. THE HEART ASKS PLEASURE FIRST
(THE PROMISE/THE SACRIFICE)

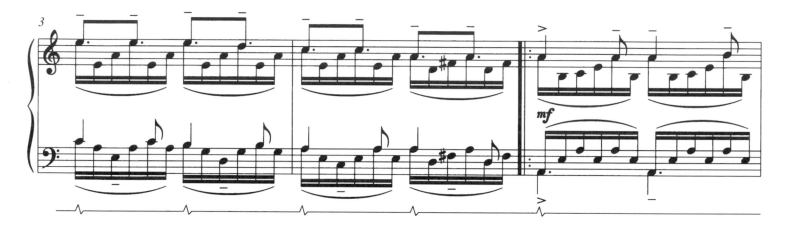

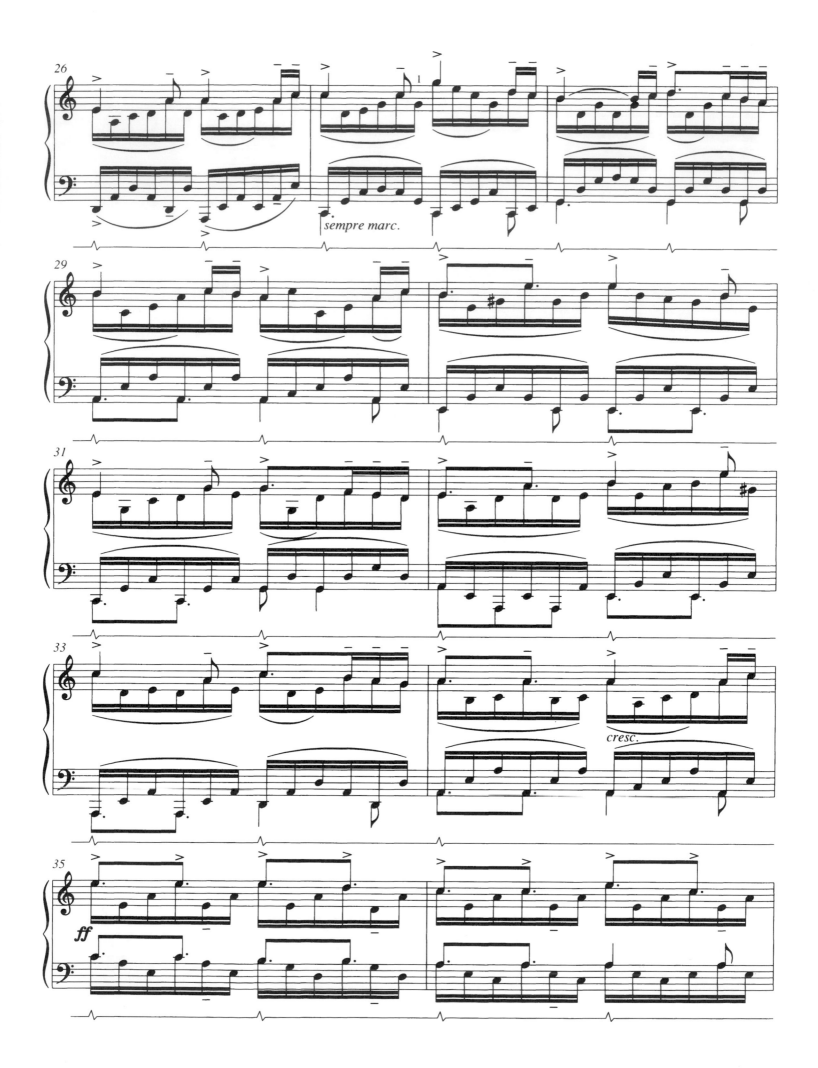

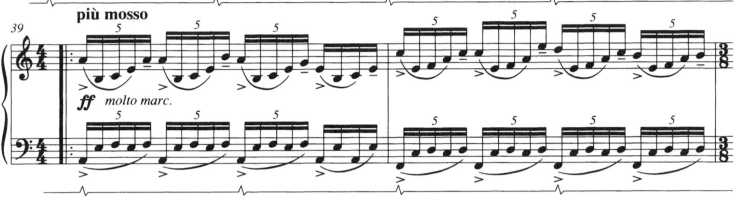

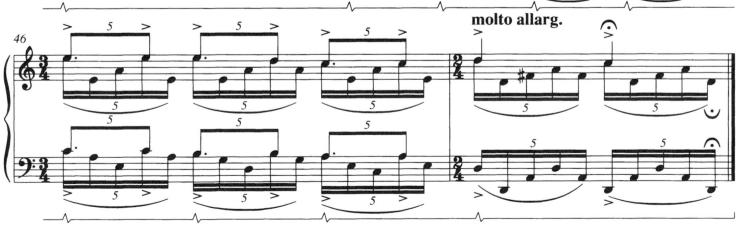

The Piano

The original six pieces
from the award-winning film
by Jane Campion.

Michael Nyman
Film Music for Solo Piano

A selection of pieces and arrangements
by the composer of his best-known film music,
plus a special collection of facsimile
reproductions of the original manuscripts.

Including music from
The Draughtsman's Contract,
Drowning by Numbers, Carrington
and *The Piano*.